"Without promotion, something terrible happens...Nothing!"
-P.T. Barnum

Sheréa VéJauan

Sheréa VéJauan

More than...101 Inexpensive and Easy Ways to Promote Your Church Event!

A Mini-Marketing Handbook for Every Church Volunteer, Ministry Leader, and Staff Member

More than...101 Inexpensive and Easy Ways to Promote Your Church Event!

A Mini-Marketing Handbook for Every Church Volunteer, Ministry Leader, and Staff Member.
Copyright©2013

Printed in the United States of America

Sheréa VéJauan
10808 Foothill Blvd, Ste. #160-260
Rancho Cucamonga, CA 91730
http://VeJauan.com/
http://101ways.vejauan.com/

Sheréa VéJauan

Table of Contents

Introduction

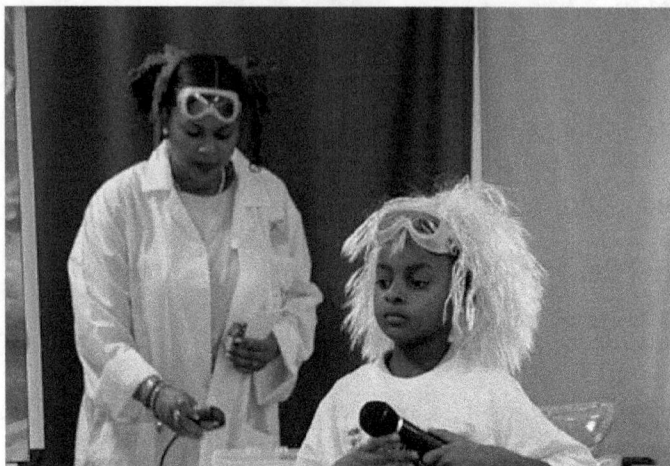

As the Children's Ministry Director of my church for over 7 years, one of my primary responsibilities was to create a clean, fun and safe environment, so that parents could enjoy their worship experience worry-free. After this was accomplished everything else was just icing on the cake - until I was reminded of one of the church's busiest holidays. Yep, you guessed it! Easter Sunday.

I grew up in church; so, I am no stranger to Easter Sunday. And I consider myself to have pretty good organizational skills, but this was significantly different.

Preparing for hundreds of families went far beyond beautiful dresses, chocolate bunnies, and baskets. I didn't expect to become an event planner, promoter, food sampler, and decorator.

I think this is true for most ministry leaders, staff members, and volunteers. We are usually pretty good at explaining our ministry plan, including curriculum, handouts, order of service, and other necessary materials for church ministry and business. However, we overlook the plan of getting the seats filled. This can be one of the most challenging tasks. Failing to put together a marketing plan can result in a waste of church resources.

"Build and they will come", carries some truths, but people have to at least know where, why, and when to show up. Having a great event scheduled does not guarantee that people will come.

An awesome, well-planned event may equal success to you. But, to church leadership, attendance will usually determine the success of the event.

A few years after serving as the Children's Ministry Director, I adopted another role at my church as the "Director of Communications and Children's Ministries". This is where I discovered two things: (1)

we need to promote our events and sermons series, and (2) we don't have a big budget.

Hence, this booklet was born. In this economy, it is my desire that the church does not get left behind. I put together this booklet to assist churches in surviving the empty-chair syndrome.

These tips are very practical, yet, many times overlooked. Most of these ideas can be implemented at no cost with a very small budget or no budget at all. I suggest meeting with your team first to decide what ideas will be most effective for your event.

Let's get started!

Sheréa VéJauan

More Than 101 Ideas

Place your event on the all-church calendar:

Most church calendars list all church meetings, classes, and events on the church's website. Talk to your church secretary or communications director about adding your event, this may include a printed and/or online version.

Send an e-blast to the church:

If the event appeals to the entire congregation -check with your pastor, communications director, IT person, or whoever is in charge, to get permission to send a church–wide email announcement.

Write an article and submit it to the newspaper:

Depending on the type of event (i.e. serving the homeless, bone barrow drive, etc.), consider writing an article and submitting it to your local newspaper. Community newspapers love local news.

Create a response email that automatically responds to people who email about your event: Talk with your IT administrator and have them set up a special email address for your event, like worshipnight@churchevents.us or vbs@churchevents.us. Once you have the email address, set up an automatic email message that responds anytime an email is sent to that address. Be sure to include a link to the event registration page.

Purchase a small advertisement in your local paper:

Place an ad in your local newspaper. Remember to ask for special discounts and/or seasonal promotions. Most newspapers, especially local newspapers have special discounts for non-profits and churches. They may also have a special religious section or church directory section that's usually set at a fixed monthly amount.

Purchase balloon clusters to add festivity to your event:
For a sure shot attention grabber, definitely consider balloons. Place balloons in various locations to use as a marker to attract, signal, or engage last minute attendees.

Hang banners outside for your event:

Banners are durable and eye catching. Because of their flexibility, they can be used in awkward places. Banners are always noticeable and attractive especially for events like Vacation Bible School.

Create bathroom signs:
Consider posting flyers behind the stalls in the bathrooms. Remember to remove them when the event is over.

Purchase a billboard advertisement:
If your budget allows, consider purchasing a billboard ad. This is a great way to let other people in your community know about the event.

Write a blog for your event:

Create a personal blog or update your church's blog with posts about your upcoming event, which will build a buzz before the event occurs. (Remember to add keywords.)

Make bookmarks:
Create and print event bookmarks for your guests to place in their bibles as reminders.

Create an information brochure:
Create a brochure that lists the details of your church event. Include FAQ's, a registration form, and other information that will be useful to your potential attendees. Be sure to include a web link for easy sign up.

Create and submit a church bulletin advertisement:

Create an ad for your event and place it in the weekly church bulletin. Don't forget to check with your communications director to see if they already have some ready-made graphics or if they'd be willing to create a nice, professional one for you.

Create a bulletin insert:

Create a half-sheet flyer and insert it inside your church bulletin.

Purchase bumper stickers:

Design and print a bumper sticker to hand out to your church ministry team and church members.

Create business card ads to hand out to potential guests:

Create a business card-sized ad about your event and pass it out. Business cards are a great way to inexpensively promote your event. They're small, affordable, and easy to hand out.

Promote your event on your church's bulletin board:

Does your church have a community board? If, so, pin up the details of your event on the bulletin board (bring some extra pins, just in case).

Advertise on ChurchEvents.US: (shameless plug)

Promote your event to thousands for just $5. Visit http://ChurchEvents.us for more info.

"Check-in" on Facebook:

When your team arrives to set-up, ask them to "check-in" on Facebook. Share a photo of your team setting up for the event. Let your potential guests know that they still have time to make it.
https://www.Facebook.com/

"Check-in" on Foursquare:

There are well-over 20 million users on Foursquare. As your guests arrive at your event, ask them to "check-in" on Foursquare. If your church has a business account, consider offering a special prize or discount offer.
http://business.foursquare.com/

Produce a free cable television show:
Create a television program based around your event and contact your local cable company. Non-profits are usually able to air their shows for free.

Create a yearly printable calendar:
Most people use a desk or wall calendar regularly in their home or office. Consider creating a calendar that your guests can use all year. Make sure to include the dates of all annual church events on the calendar as an easy reminder.

Create coffee sleeves:
Most people come to church with a Bible in one hand and coffee in the other (I know I do). If your church has a coffee bar, consider investing in coffee sleeves.

When it comes close to your event, use these in your church's cafeteria or wherever coffee is served.

Promote your event on college and university campuses:

If your event appeals to college and/or university students, consider speaking with the schools faculty to see how you can advertise your event. Schools generally have their own radio stations and newspapers. You should also try to contact the company in charge of the billboard ads on campus.

Submit your event to community events calendars:

Contact your local newspaper. Most papers have a community calendar section and will include your event for free.

Call your local Christian radio station:

Contact your local Christian radio stations and ask about commercial rates or information on Public Service Announcements (PSA's). Some Christian radio stations or even secular stations may also have a community calendar segment.

Magnetic Car Signs:

Purchase magnetic car signs and have your team drive around with them on their cars until your event is over.

Secure a local celebrity to host or speak:

Consider getting a local celebrity, an athlete from a major league team, a politician, or anyone who has a huge influence in the community to host or speak at your event. They usually have fans that will come to your event just to see them.

Join your local Chamber of Commerce and get involved:
If your church is a member of your local Chamber, contact them for assistance in promoting your event. They usually produce a monthly newsletter, allowing you to insert flyers in their printed newsletters, promote at mixers, and a lot more. They even provide mailing lists and labels for a small fee. If you are not a member... join immediately! http://www.chamberfind.com/

Conduct classes or workshops:
Create a class or workshop around your event with the last class ending on the day of the event.

Create a coloring contest for the for the neighborhood kids:

Display all of the entries in the main entrance area of the event and give a prize to the winner.

Use community bulletin boards:

Print flyers and place them on local community bulletin boards. These are usually located in coffee shops and grocery stores.

Use Constant Contact's email/event service:

If you have an account with <u>Constant Contact</u>, create a Constant Contact event email. This is a great program to RSVP, track guests, and print tickets. For more information on Constant Contact, visit <u>http://www.constantcontact.com/index.jsp?pn=realisticallyspeaking</u>

Have a contest to get others involved and excited about your event:

Create a fun contest within the event such as: best costume, best dance, or karaoke sing-off. Get creative.

Wear costumes:

While promoting your event, consider wearing a funny hat or costume. This will bring lots of attention to your event.

Place an ad on Craig's List:

List your event at http://craigslist.org

Send out direct mail pieces:
This could get a little pricey. However if it's worth it to you, start way in advance. Being a non-profit, you should be able to apply for a special postage.
https://www.usps.com/business/send-mail-for-business.htm

Go Door-to Door:
Promote your event door-to-door, on your street, apartment building, or the surrounding neighborhood where your church is located. This is also a great way to meet the neighbors.

Promote your event with door hangers:
Design, print, and distribute door hangers in the community where your church is located. Check with your city to see if you need permission or a permit.

Create a download section on your church website:

Make it easy for your future attendees to download info ahead of time, like maps, flyers, and registration forms.

Create a promotional DVD:

You can include a special message from the pastor or the event coordinator, show photos from last year's event, add music, and more.

Place a flyer in the church elevator:

Make good use of your church elevator by placing flyers inside. This makes for a great conversation piece on the way up or down.

Create an eMail tagline:

Add an email tag line at the end of your email signature. Don't forget to add a link to the event registration page.

Send an Evite:

With more than 22 million registered users and over 25,000 invitations sent each hour, Evite is the top online invitation and social planning website. Electronic invitations are free to send and receive. So you save on stamps and trees. They also have an app that links to Facebook and other social media networks. http://www.evite.com

Create a Facebook ad:

Get started at:
https://www.Facebook.com/advertising

Create a Facebook event:

Create a Facebook event page under your church's "Fan Page". Your guests can also "share" and "like" your event with their friends and family.
https://www.Facebook.com/events/list

Create a FAQ's list:

Answer questions ahead of time about parking, childcare, and other event related questions would help your guests make up their mind about attending your event.

Make a flyer:

Don't underestimate the standard event flyer. You can make a full sheet or half-size. You can also upload it to your webpage in PDF format and let your guests download it and/or forward it to their friends. It saves ink and the planet. I use Scribd to upload my PDF documents and then link them to my website. http://www.scribd.com/svejauan

Serve food or refreshments: Consider having food at your event and advertise it ahead of time. People love food, whether it's free or if there is a small cost. This one thing alone could increase your audience. Having food may also encourage your guests to stay longer. There's nothing worse than having hunger pains when you are trying to enjoy an event.

Ask confirmed and potential guests to bring and invite others:

Encourage your congregation and/or registered guests to bring a friend to the event. This one idea could double your event – literally.

Have giveaways:

Consider giving away a prize or two, maybe a big prize giveaway like an iPad or flat screen TV. Promote the giveaway on your advertisements.

Create a Google Ad:

Create a Google ad at http://www.google.com/ads/

Invite Groups:

Inviting a group to your event like a community choir or Girl Scout troop. Your events fill up quicker when big groups attend.

Be a "Groupie" by promoting to your personal and professional email groups:

If you are a member of any online groups, such as mom group, online community groups, or Facebook groups, by all means invite them. Make sure you check with the group administrator to make sure you are not violating any solicitation rules.

Create an informational voice message for callers on hold:

If your church's phone system has an "on hold" feature, add your event details. You can also pre-record a message and members can listen when they call the church office during "off" hours.

Invite People:

This sounds silly, but it is so true. You'd be surprised at how many churches print flyers and build websites, but never personally invite guests. Get on the phone and do it the old-fashioned way - call people or just ask them face-to-face.

Make Invite Cards:

Create invite cards for your church members to hand out to their friends and family.

Use Internet promotion companies:

Use Internet publicity companies to send out special announcements or press releases online. They usually charge between $99-$200 to send out an eblast to their eList.

Set-up an information table:

Place your flyers on the info table at your church. If your church does not have one, ask if you can set up one each Sunday until the end of your event. You should also consider setting up an information booth at another church ministry event. Most likely, the same audience in attendance may also be interested in attending your event.

Hold a kick–off event:

About one week before your event, get the people excited about what they should expect by hosting a kick-off event.

Use your mailing list:

Don't forget to use last year's mailing list. The guests that enjoyed your event last year are waiting to come back.

Media Release:

Send a media release to local newspapers.
http://www.christiannewswire.com/

Media room:

Set up a media room on your church's website. Include things like your media release, high-resolution graphics and photos or anything else the media might use to help write a great article about your event.

Use Meet UP:

If your church sponsors ongoing community events like MOPS, consider using Meetup.com. Meet up is the world's largest network of local groups. More than 9,000 groups get together in local communities each day.
http://www.meetup.com

Ministry Fair:

Promote your event at your church's next ministry fair. Ministry fairs are designed to help ministries recruit new volunteers and share information about their ministry. How about including a flyer for your next ministry event? Even if members are not interested in joining your ministry right now, they may be interested in attending your next recital, luncheon, or get together. So at the next ministry fair, don't just think "recruitment" think relationship.

Ministry Invite:

If there is a cost for your event, consider contacting other ministries in your church and offer them a ministry discount if they bring their team members. Offer the group leader a free ticket as a "thank-you" in exchange for "x" amount of tickets sold.

Create a movie theatre ad for your event:

Visit your local movie theatre and find out how you can run an ad on the movie screen. Usually, outside companies handle these requests, but the manager will be able to refer you to them.

Send out newsletters:
Create an event newsletter either before or after your event. If your church already prints and distributes a newsletter, ask if your event can be highlighted.

Network with other churches:
Partner or co-sponsor your events with other churches and community groups around the neighborhood. This is a great way to get to know other organizations, as well as using the opportunity to pull resources together to make the event more successful.

Promote next year's event...this year:
If this is an annual event, check your calendar and come up with next year's

date. Print a save the date flyer and consider promoting next year's event at this year's event.

Online radio promotion:
Online radio shows hosts are always looking for guests and filler advertisements. Check out Blog Talk Radio (http://www.blogtalkradio.com/) and use the "search" feature to find shows that have an audience who are interested in your event. Be a host in exchange for free advertisement.

Create your own online radio show:
Consider starting an entire online radio show around your event. Interview the featured speakers or musical guests that

will be at your event. Offer a few giveaways.

Write personalized letters to your potential guests:

Pull out the old Rolodex and send out personalized letters to your friends, family and people who you'd love to see at your event. State how important it will be when they show up.

Make phone calls:

Sure, it takes a little more time, but it's more personal than a text message or email.

Take lots of photos:

Please make sure you have a designated photographer to take photos at your

event. Afterwards, post them on all of
your social media sites. Even though the
event is over, this is your opportunity to
show those who didn't make it the fun
they missed. After seeing your photos,
they'll be sure not to miss your next
event.

Posters:
Create posters of your event and
distribute them throughout the
neighborhood or local shops.

Postcards:
Create postcards and distribute them to
the addresses in your church's database.

Power Point Presentations:
Create power point presentations you can
show at the next church service or
ministry event.

Have a raffle:

Guests love raffles! Consider having a raffle at your event. Let your guests know ahead of time about the raffle. If your church has a bigger budget, use some if it to buy a huge prize like an iPod or TV and raffle it off to ticket buyers. Use this as an incentive to increase ticket sales.

Refrigerator magnets:

Print refrigerator magnets that your potential guests can place on the fridge as a reminder about your upcoming event.

"Save The Date" cards:

Don't yet have all the details about your event? Create "save the date" cards with just the date and a web address that your potential guests can check for updated info.

Skit:

Promote your event during Sunday services by having your ministry team perform a skit.

Sky writing:

This form of mobile advertising is interactive, captivating, and easily targeted for stadiums, beaches, concerts, and sporting events.

Souvenir book:

Schools and community groups always have events, and most produce an annual souvenir or yearbook to help raise additional funds for their future projects. Consider purchasing an ad or two. It also shows your commitment and support to the community.

Speak up: Are you a speaker?

Do you have a few months or even a year before your event comes up? Volunteer to speak at a few local gatherings with an option to set up a booth to promote your event.

Staff meetings:

I can't tell you how many times I sat in staff meetings and never knew half the stuff other people on my team were doing until I read an announcement in the bulletin. Start promoting your event to your immediate team. You may find out that they can help you with a few tasks of pulling off the event. Get your event on every internal staff and ministry leader calendar.

Street team:

Hire or put together a volunteer street team to help you get the word out.

Taxi cabs & buses:

Taxi advertising is one of the strongest ways to get ads in front of a traveling, commuting, or conference-attending audience.

T-shirts:

Consider getting t-shirts printed with graphics and details of your event. Remember to include the web address. You can also give away t-shirts as raffle items or early bird registration gifts (i.e. the first 100 registrants will get a free t-shirt).

Text messages:

Send reminder text messages a few days before and the day of the event. Make sure you get permission.

Twitter hashtag:

If you already have a Twitter account, create a Twitter hashtag for your event. Ask your guests to Tweet about the event while they are there (i.e. #churchbbq, #worshipnight).

Vendor booth:

Consider having vendor booths at your event. This creates buzz from the expectant vendors. They will tell their faithful clients to support them at your event, plus it will allow you to raise some extra cash as you charge for the booth rental space.

Verbal announcement:

Have your pastor make a verbal announcement from the pulpit (these have always seemed to work best for most church events).

Video commercial:

Create a quick video trailer about your church's event and post it on YouTube, Facebook, your website or other video sites like Vimeo and GodTube.

Voice blast:

Create a voice blast that goes out to everyone on your phone list. Although it's not as personal, it sure saves lots of time by not having to call everyone individually. Or, you can make this your initial call and follow up with a personal call a few days later.

Web banner:

Have your tech guy (or girl) create a web banner ad with an html code, and post it on the "download section" of your event page. Encourage the business owners in your church to consider placing the banner ad on their company's site.

Web page and/or post:

Create a webpage on your church's website that has a download section for your potential guests to download flyers, videos, maps, FAQ's, etc.

Web site:

If your event is annual, consider building an entire website geared around the event. You can include info about the upcoming event, registration forms, testimonials, and photos from previous years.

Word of mouth:

The single best way to get the word out about your event is still word of mouth. Tell your friends to tell their friends about your upcoming event.

Yard signs:

Place yard signs in a 1-mile radius of the church property, if appropriate, tie some balloons to the signs).

Set-up a video area for testimonials and feedback about your event:

Set up a video camera in a quiet corner of the room at your event. Ask your guests to leave a quick 20-30 second testimonial about the event. Upload the finished videos to your website, YouTube channel and all of your social media sites. NOTE: **Prepare a few questions ahead of**

time to make the time flow little easier. You may also want to have a stack of photo/video release forms available for your guests to sign.

Bonus Ideas

Thank your guests:

After your event, thank your guests. Let them know it was because of them that your event was successful. Use this "Thank you" opportunity to invite them to fill out your event survey and invite them to next year's event.

Thank your team:

Teamwork makes the dream work! (That's my philosophy.) After your event is over, send a handwritten thank you note or a small gift to your team. As an extra-added touch, send a photo of them helping out at the event. Or (with permission) upload the photos to Facebook and "tag" them in it to let the world know how awesome they are. They'll be happy to help you again in the future. Remember, you can't have a successful event without a great team.

Surveys:

The one thing I hate to love. There's nothing worse than assuming your event was successful, yet your guests were disappointed. Although the event is over, giving your guests a voice will let them know that you care and that you are always striving for a better experience.

Tickets:

Tickets can be used for more than just an entrance to your event. Include your church's web address or consider having a business sponsor the back of the ticket with an ad.

YouTube:

Create a YouTube account, record and add videos related to your upcoming event. https://www.youtube.com/

Hootsuite:

Use Hootsuite to schedule messages about your upcoming event. https://hootsuite.com/

Instagram:

Use Instagram to capture photo highlights and ask your guests to tag your church and use a hashtag. You can log on to Instagram later to see photos that you would have normally never had the opportunity to see. http://instagram.com/

Recap video:

Have your team create a video of the highlights of your event. You can use this video footage to promote your event for next year.

Hand out small gifts:
Purchase some small gifts, candy, or treats that are related to your event and hand them out along with a flyer or invite card.

Podcasts:
Talk to your IT staff members at church to see if they can help you create a podcast. It's an audio broadcast available as an MP3 file that you can play on a portable music player, such as an iPod, or on a computer.
http://www.apple.com/itunes/podcasts/specs.html

Promotional items:
If you have a budget, find a few promotional items that are most appropriate for your event and order away.

Get a QR code:
http://www.scanlife.com/

Get a few sponsors for your event.
This will help draw more people to your event while generating extra cash.

Yearly Campaigns to Consider when Planning Your Church Events

In addition to planning and promoting your church events, consider adding some of these yearly campaigns by partnering with other non-profits and organizations. Most of these campaigns include marketing ideas and sample templates to help you get a jumpstart on your promotions. Here are some of my favorites:

Samaritan's Purse's Shoe Box Drive
http://www.samaritanspurse.org/

Back to Church Sunday
http://backtochurch.com

Angel Tree
http://www.prisonfellowship.org/programs/angel-tree

SOUPer Bowl Sunday
http://souperbowl.org

Harvest America
http://harvest.org

Weekend to remember
http://www.familylife.com/events/featured-events/weekend-to-remember

One Warm Coat Drive

http://onewarmcoat.org/

Trunk or Treat

A Trunk or Treat is a Halloween event that is often church- or community-sponsored. People gather and park their cars in a large parking lot. They open their trunks, or the backs of their vehicles, and decorate them. Then they pass out candy from their trunks. The event provides a safe family environment for trick or treaters.

Big Sunday

http://bigsunday.org/

My Church's Annual Events

Use these next pages to list annual community events in your area that you can host or participate in.

January

_____

_____

_____

February

_____

_____

_____

March

_____

_____

_____

April

_____

_____

_____

May

_____

_____

_____

June

_____

_____

_____

July

_____

_____

_____

August

_____

_____

_____

September

_____

_____

_____

October

_____
_____
_____

November

_____
_____
_____

December

_____
_____
_____

Sherea VéJauan's Favorites: Resource List

Social Media Resources:

Facebook: http://www.facebook.com/

FourSquare: https://foursquare.com/

Hootsuite: https://hootsuite.com/

Instagram: http://instagram.com/

Twitter: https://Twitter.com/

WordPress: http://wordpress.com/

YouTube: http://www.youtube.com/

Outsourcing Resources:

99 designs: http://99designs.com/

Fiveer.com: http://fiverr.com/

Elance: https://www.elance.com/

Graphic Resources:

PicMonkey: http://www.picmonkey.com/

BeFunky: http://www.befunky.com/

99 designs: http://99designs.com/

iStock Photo: http://www.istockphoto.com/

Easily Creates Graphics Like the Pros w/ Logo Creator: http://wp.me/P11FCr-6f

Event Promotion Resources:

(California) Full calendar http://sfbayarea.fullcalendar.com/

Church Event Promotion: http://churchevents.us

Christian Happenings: http://www.christianhappenings.com/

http://VéJauan.com/in the news/

Enewsletters:

Constant Contact: Invest in a program like Constant Contact to send email campaigns, manage events, and create surveys and more. To sign up, go to: http://churcheventpromotion.com/promote-your-church-event/enewsletter/

Mail Chimp: http://mailchimp.com/

iContact: http://www.icontact.com/

Aweber: http://www.aweber.com/

Print Resources:

Print Safari: http://www.printsafari.com/

Vista print: http://www.vistaprint.com/

Easy Design Software:

Microsoft Publisher for PC:
http://www.microsoftstore.com/

Pages for Mac: http://www.apple.com/iwork/pages/

Microsoft Word templates: (free online):
http://office.microsoft.com/en-us/templates/

Helpful Websites:

Church Marketing Sucks:
http://www.churchmarketingsucks.com

Outreach Magazine: http://www.outreach.com/

http://www.effectivechurchcom.com/

http://churchtechtoday.com/

http://www.rsistewardship.com/

www.Lynda.com.com

Church juice http://churchjuice.com/

Goodwill Communications helps non-profit organizations and government agencies develop and distribute public service advertising campaigns that further their critical mission. To learn more, click on the orange bar beneath each of the case histories. http://www.psaresearch.com/

Advertise:

Craig's list: http://craigslist.org/

Press Release:

Christian News Wire: http://www.christiannewswire.com/

PR Web: http://www.prweb.com/

Blog Resources:

WordPress: http://wordpress.com

Blogger: http://www.blogger.com/

Church Calendars:

Church Calendars:http://www.mychurchevents.com/

Google Calendar: https://www.google.com/calendar

Video Resources:

GodTube: http://www.godtube.com/

You Tube: https://www.youtube.com/

Vimeo: https://vimeo.com/

Food/Refreshments:

Costco: http://www.costco.com/

Sam's Club: http://www.samsclub.com/

Dollar Tree: http://www.dollartree.com/

99 Cents Store: http://www.99only.com/

Other:

Blog talk radio: http://www.blogtalkradio.com/

Brown bags: http://www.brownpapertickets.com/

Café press: http://www.cafepress.com/

Chamber of Commerce:
http://www.chamberfind.com/

Coffee Sleeves http://www.printglobe.com/

Coffee Sleeves:
http://coffeesleevemojo.com/store/custom-cup-sleeves-two-sided-church-discount

Custom Ink: T-shirts http://www.customink.com/

Direct Mail: https://www.usps.com/business/send-mail-for-business.htm

Doc Stoc: http://www.docstoc.com/

Eventbrite: http://eventbrite.com/

Evite: http://new.evite.com/

Google ads: http://www.google.com/ads/

KKLA: http://www.kkla.com/

MeetUP: http://www.meetup.com

Oriental Trading: Promo items, raffle prizes, tickets, etc.: http://www.orientaltrading.com/

Party City: http://www.partycity.com/

Punch Tab: https://www.punchtab.com/

Scba: http://SCbA.com/

Scribd: http://www.scribd.com/

Sky Writing: http://theskywriters.com/

Speakermatch: http://www.speakermatch.com/

Survey Monkey: http://www.surveymonkey.com/

Taxi Cabs: http://www.bluelinemedia.com/

Tee shirts: http://www.customink.com/

Tickets: http://www.itickets.com/

Trumphia: Text messaging http://trumpia.com/

Voice blast: http://www.voiceshot.com/

Webs: http://www.webs.com/

Wix: http://www.wix.com/

Zazzle: http://www.zazzle.com/

http://partycentral.orientaltrading.com/signup

http://www.ministrybox.org/

Screen Vision: www.screenvision.com

Visit http://churchevents.us often, as we will be adding more content, video and resources with each tip provided here in this booklet.

The List:

1. Place your event on the all-church calendar
2. Send an e-blast to the church
3. Write an article and submit it to the newspaper
4. Create an response email that automatically responds to people who email about your event
5. Purchase a small advertisement in your local paper
6. Purchase balloon clusters to add festivity to your event
7. Purchase banners to hang outside for your event
8. Create bathroom signs
9. Purchase a billboard advertisement
10. Write a blog for your event
11. Make bookmarks
12. Create an information brochure
13. Create and submit a church bulletin advertisement
14. Create a bulletin insert
15. Purchase bumper stickers
16. Create business-sized card advertisements to hand out to potential guests

17. Promote your event on your church's bulletin board
18. Advertise on ChurchEvents.US
19. "Check-in" on Facebook
20. Check-in on Foursquare
21. Produce a free cable television show
22. Create a yearly printable calendar
23. Create coffee sleeves
24. Promote your event on college and university campuses
25. Submit your event to community events calendars
26. Call your local Christian radio station
27. Magnetic car signs
28. Secure a local celebrity to host or speak
29. Join your local chamber of commerce and get involved
30. Conduct classes or workshops
31. Create a coloring contest for the for the neighborhood kids
32. Use community bulletin boards
33. Use Constant Contact's email/event service
34. Have a contest to get others involved and excited about your event
35. Wear costumes
36. Place an ad on Craig's List

37. Send out direct mail pieces
38. Go door-to-door
39. Promote your event with door hangers
40. Create a download section on your church website
41. Create a promotional DVD
42. Place a flyer in the church elevator
43. Create an eMail tagline
44. Send an Evite
45. Create a Facebook ad
46. Create a Facebook event
47. Create a FAQ's list
48. Make a flyer
49. Serve food or refreshments
50. Ask confirmed and potential guests to bring and invite others
51. Have giveaways
52. Create a Google ad
53. Invite groups
54. Be a "groupie" by promoting to your personal and professional email groups
55. Create an informational voice message for callers on hold
56. Invite people
57. Make invite cards
58. Use Internet promotion companies

59.   Set-up an information table
60.   Hold a kick –off event
61.   Use your mailing list
62.   Media release
63.   Media room
64.   Use Meet UP
65.   Ministry fair
66.   Ministry invite
67.   Create a movie theatre ad for your event
68.   Send out newsletters
69.   Network with other churches
70.   Promote next year's event…this year
71.   Online radio promotion
72.   Create your own online radio show
73.   Write personalized letters to your potential guests
74.   Make phone calls
75.   Take lots of photos
76.   Posters
77.   Postcards
78.   Power Point presentations
79.   Have a raffle
80.   Refrigerator magnets
81.   "Save the Date" cards
82.   Skit
83.   Sky writing

84. Souvenir book

85. Speak up: Are you a speaker?

86. Staff meetings

87. Street team

88. Taxi cabs & buses

89. T-shirts

90. Text messages

91. Twitter hash tag

92. Vendor booth

93. Verbal announcement

94. Video commercial

95. Voice blast

96. Web banner

97. Web page and/or post

98. Web site

99. Word of mouth

100. Yard sign

101. Set-up a video area for testimonials and feedback about your event

Sheréa is a published author, vocalist, and professional freelance writer. She is also the co-founder of The Goal Setter's Club, a coaching organization based in Rancho Cucamonga, California, that introduces the art of goal setting to America's youth.

Believing in excellence, Sheréa continues to hone her craft as a poet and vocalist as a member of the American Society of Composers, Authors, and Publishers, the Christian Writer's Guild of San Diego County, and Toastmasters International.

Sheréa is author of several book titles, including, *Realistically Speaking: Speaking What's Real, Keeping What's Holy*.

Sheréa resides in Southern California, devoted wife for over twenty-two years to her husband Brian, and mother to their three children, Reginald, Jasmyn and Kennedy.

Other Books By Sheréa VéJauan

5 Easy Steps on How to Get Your Events in the News!: http://VéJauan.com/inthenews/

My Physical Health & Fitness Journal: http://VéJauan.com/fitnessjournal/

Everything You Need to Know about Pinterest: http://VéJauan.com/pinterest/

Goals Journal. Write.Balance.Celebrate: http://VéJauan.com/goalsjournal/

How to Make or Save Money with Fiverr.com: http://VéJauan.com/makemoneywithfiverr/

Realistically Speaking: http://vejauan.com/realisticallyspeaking/

Connect:

Website: http://VéJauan.com
Twitter: https://twitter.com/shereavejauan
Facebook: https://www.facebook.com/VeJauan
Scribd: http://www.scribd.com/svejauan

My Notes:

_____

_____

_____

_____

_____

_____

_____

_____

_____

_____

_____

_____

_____

_____

_____

_____

_____

_____

_____

www.ingramcontent.com/pod-product-compliance
Lightning Source LLC
Chambersburg PA
CBHW050557280326
41933CB00011B/1877